Introduction

These Everlasting Cake recipes grew out of my love for baking and a passion for image making. Here are cakes, biscuits, pies and sweetmeats collected over a number of years from all over the world. For fun, some of the recipes tie in with events on the calendar. All of them have been tried and tested, and some have a history or anecdote attached which you may find entertaining. Above all, this is an occupational therapy book of fun stuff to do in the kitchen — a tactile experience of mushing together a variety of ingredients using a proven scientific formula, creating something enjoyable and impressive to eat (selfishly alone, or to share with loved ones)!

I know there is a move to be healthier and eat more carrot sticks, however life demands that there must also be some fun and enjoyment and the glories of cake creation provide a perfect opportunity to indulge. I advise that only the best ingredients are used — avoid horror E numbers, colourants and supermarket bicarb aftertaste preservatives. Indulge in a moderate way, try one cake per week or just whenever you feel like something sweet and special to dip into. Beating up a cake can be good in so many ways, and eating and sharing simply prolongs this pleasure. Revel in the alchemy that takes place in the kitchen!

These are no fuss recipes and as for any mess, in the words of a dear friend who lives on the opposite side of the world, "licking the bowl is good for the soul."

It is not my intention to intimidate anyone with glossy photographs of glycerine laden foods, but rather to present a different perspective on fabulous food making — a serving suggestion rather than a prescription on how your creation may look and taste.

Enjoy!

Kathy

Hints

Turn oven on before you start so it reaches correct temperature.

Prepare tin/pans first so batter is not left standing and air escapes causing cake to be flat.

Baking parchment or reusable baking silicone is my preferred lining as greaseproof is a bit flimsy

Use organic large fresh eggs wherever possible.

Break eggs into a separate bowl, in case not fresh. Ditto when separating to ensure no egg yolk mixes with the white.

Always use a clean non greasy bowl when whisking egg whites.

Use good quality pure vanilla extract over standard vanilla essence.

Cut corners whenever you can — buy pastry/make lining templates/lick the bowl/cut off burnt bits and cover with icing/use spray and cook or other for greasing.

I apologise that some of the recipes are in cup measurements and others are in grams — these are the way they have been given to me and in the spirit of the book have decided to keep them in as original form as possible. I confess to converting the lbs and oz's.

Tsp = teaspoon

Tbs = tablespoon

6 = gram weight

Cup = standard measuring cup

Oven settings are for regular centigrade ovens, reduce slightly for fan assisted ovens

Everlasting Recipes

Weekly suggestions

1   Bolo Rei
2   Poppy Seed Cake
3   Apple Strudel
4   Meringues
5   Treacle Tart
6   Lemon Brulée
7   Chocolate Heart Cake
8   Baked Cheese Cake
9   Pancakes
10   Pastéis de Nata
11   Chocolate Cherry Muffins
12   Scones
13   Marvellous Marble Cake
14   Banana Cake
15   Almond Easter Cake
16   Dalmatian Brix
17   Flapjacks
18   Mom's Lemon Loaf
19   Red Wine Chocolate Cake
20   Mousse Chocolate
21   Wedding Cake
22   Halva Cake
23   Oat Bran Muffins
24   Apfelkuchen
25   Boozy Cointreau and Marmalade Cake
26   White Chocolate Cheesecake

27   Jam Tart
28   Lemon Meringue Pie
29   Chilli Slices
30   Sprinkle Sandwich
31   Broa Castellar
32   Peanut Butter Cookies
33   Birthday Cake
34   Carrot Cake
35   Shirley's Shortbread
36   Ginger Cake
37   Apple and Blackberry Oat Crumble
38   Boiled Fruit Cake
39   Classic Trifle
40   Black Forest Gâteaux
41   Dreamy Creamy Apple Cake
42   Victoria Sponge
43   Strawberry White Port Meringue
44   Super Chocolate Salami
45   Citrus Water Sponge
46   Jen's Parev Chocolate Cake
47   Mini Pumpkin Pies
48   George's Glorious Jam Loaf
49   Marshmallow Crispies
50   Butter Iced Cupcakes
51   Extraordinary Xmas Cake
52   Pudim Flan

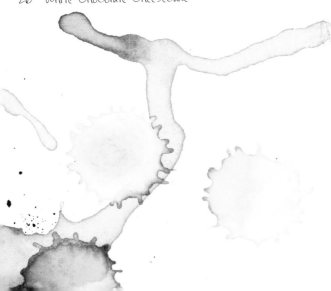

Bolo Rei

Bolo Rei — or Kings Cake is a traditional Portuguese celebration cake. It is shared on the 12th night Christmas amongst family and friends and apart from its majestic bejewelling of candied fruits it contains a special secret — a Fava (or dried bean), and sometimes as with Christmas pud — charm as well. The fun of the Fava is that the person receiving a slice of Bolo Rei containing the bean is blessed with good luck and is responsible for the provision of the cake for the following year — thu ensuring the tradition has continuity and the expense is shared! I love Bolo Rei — it looks so gra and regal, and above all tastes delicious — bom apetite.

This is a recipe for a big cake as it is shared with all — if you think it may be too much, halve the ingredients. As with all yummy things — this is a bit time consuming. You need to begin the night be

250g mixed dried fruit and nuts
(include raisins, sultanas, pine nuts and nuts)
50ml Port wine or aguardente (Portuguese fire water)

Zest of 1 lemon and 1 orange

1tsp sugar

100ml warm milk

150g castor sugar

4 eggs

125g butter cubed

Coloured Glacé Cherries

Coloured sugar crystals

Extra flour for hands

1 sachet yeast (25g)

60ml warm water

625g flour

1g salt

1 yolk beaten for brushing

Whole glacé fruits

Candied peel

Warm smooth apricot jam for glaze

1 or 2 Fava (dried broad beans)

Set nuts aside. Steep fruit overnight in port or aguardente till swollen and all alcohol absorbed.

The next day. Dissolve yeast with the tsp sugar in 60ml warm water. Sprinkle with 1tbs flour, place in a warm draught free place to form a spongy surface — when flour cracks it is ready (about 20 — 30 m

Beat eggs, sugar, salt and zest. Add yeast mixture and gradually knead in flour, lastly add butter cube by cube. Knead really well to a smooth elastic consistency that does not stick to your hands. Keep dusting hands with extra flour to prevent stickiness.

Cover with a nearly dry, damp cloth and put aside to rise for 3 — 4 hours in a warm draught free pl

Set oven at 180° when dough has doubled in quantity. Prepare a parchment or silicone lined baking tra

Knead in nuts and soaked fruit mixture. Shape dough into one huge crown or two smaller ones. Plunge Fava bean deeply into each crown and cover hole.

Brush with beaten egg yolk and decorate like a crown with glacé fruit, sugar crystals, cherries and candied peel.

Bake for 30 — 40 minutes till just brown. Place on a baking rack and immediately brush with apricot glaze. If warmed apricot is a bit thick, add a small amount of water when heating.

This is delicious warm, and will keep for up to a week especially if you spread slices with butter. Good luck and don't break your teeth on the Fava!

1

Poppy Seed Cake

This has to be the easiest-peasiest cake to make: practically all the ingredients are chucked in at the same time, and then bunged into the oven!

3 cups self raising flour
1½ cups sugar
4 eggs
1 cup orange juice
(I use the lunch box packs or juice two fresh oranges)
1 tsp good vanilla essence
4 tsp baking powder
½ tsp salt
250g butter
100g poppy seeds

Turn oven onto 180°. Grease and line donut cake tin.

Mix till a smooth batter all the ingredients, except the poppy seeds.

Gently fold in poppy seeds.

Bake for about 45 mins, until crust is brown and knife comes out clean when tested.

When cooled, dust generously with sieved icing sugar.

Delicious, enjoy your poppy seed smile!

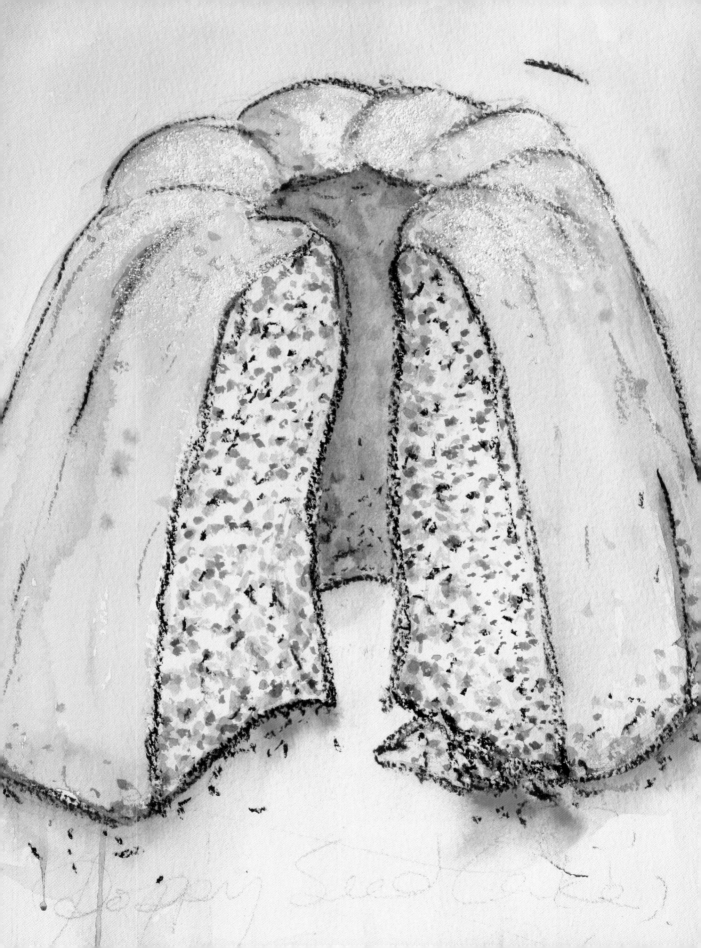

Apple Strudel

Your friends will faint when you proudly present this strudel — little knowing that it has taken less than 15 minutes to prepare!

1 packet ready made filo pastry (defrosted)

At least 125g melted butter

Large can of pie apples (or freshly cubed cooking apples if you prefer)

Handful of raisins — optional

Handful of pecan or walnuts

Vanilla sugar

Icing sugar, sieved for decoration

Cream or ice cream to serve

Heat oven according to instructions on filo packet — this should be about 190°.

On the lined baking tray you will use for cooking, thoroughly brush the sheets of filo pastry with melted butter. Upon completion they should form a neat pile over the baking sheet.

Empty can of pie apples along 1/3 line of the pastry, scatter nuts and raisins — mixing gently with a fork. Sprinkle with vanilla sugar to taste. Roll up pastry and apple mix tucking in ends before last roll. Flip over so that edge is underneath the strudel. Score diagonally three of four times with a sharp knife.

Place in oven and bake according to filo packet instructions — about ½ hour, till golden brown.

When cooked, slide off baking sheet and dust with sieved icing sugar.

Delicious warm or cool, with or without cream or ice cream.

Take a bow!

3

Meringues

An ideal way of using up egg white from yolk only recipes like pastéis de nata or cheesecake.

I love huge voluptuous cowpat meringues, and prefer individual blobs to an uncuttable Pavlova. Served on a dish piled precariously high, they look awesomely impressive!

The basic quantity is as follows:

4 egg whites

1 cup castor sugar

Coloured sugar sprinkles or granulated sugar (optional)

Extrapolate from this according to your number of egg whites.

Set oven to 140°, and prepare trays. If you can access the wondrous silicone baking paper it is marvellous for meringue making. At no time should any fat get near the mixture, so greased baking sheets are a no-no. The silicone allows meringues to slip off easily when cooked and you use it over and over (mine goes in the dishwasher). Otherwise line with parchment or greaseproof paper.

In a spotlessly clean bowl beat egg whites till stiff peaks, (but not breaking up). Whilst still beating gently pour castor sugar until mixed. Some cooks will add the tiniest pinch of salt as they find th ensures crispy meringues. (I like mine gooey in the middle). Dollop tablespoons of the meringue mixture onto baking sheets, swirl to peak, add sprinkles/sugar if required and bake for about an hour. Turn off oven and leave in the oven for at least four hours, preferably overnight before removing. This helps to dry out the meringue. Serve with seasonal fruit, cream, ice cream or ju on their own.

Treacle Tart

Treacle Tart is a hit and miss little pie — one loves it or hates it — and considering it is made primarily of stale breadcrumbs, lashings of treacle and ready roll pastry it's no wonder.
Again a very easy thing to make and as it is made up as one goes along, the exact quantities do not really matter. You can even decide if you want a deep filled tart or an elegant sliver of a. Word of warning — don't eat just out of the oven, the treacle has been known to leave third degre burns on the palate.

White breadcrumbs (no mould please) — can be made by whizzing slices of bread up in a food processor or grating, using a box food grater. You will need about 3 — 4 cups

Treacle — if it is not runny enough stand the tin in some boiling water whilst you prepare breadcrum

Ready made short crust pastry — defrosted

Lemon zest — optional

Double cream — ditto

Turn oven temperature on according to ready made pastry packaging — about 190°. Line pastry dish with the pastry, including the sides and over the edges. Secure by pressing a fork all around the edges, and down the sides if you like.

Place breadcrumbs in a large bowl and add enough runny treacle to just coat all the crumbs.
Mix thoroughly and that's it — spoon into the waiting pastry case. For variety you may want to add few teaspoons of lemon zest — this takes the very sweet edge off the tart. Also a good dollup of dout cream works wonders to improve consistency, increase calorific value and adds a wonderful caramel flavour to your dish. Bake in the oven for 20 minutes or till pastry and treacle mixture browns.

It is lovely served with vanilla ice cream or whipped cream, just warm.

Retro memory lane..............

Lemon brulée

My friends cross continents when they hear Lemon Brulée is on the menu.
What they do not know is how amazingly simple a recipe it is, but I don't mind telling if they ask!

400g ginger biscuits — crushed (the best ones are those with ginger bits)

100g melted butter

400g cream cheese (full fat only or it wont set)

200g fromage frais (full fat only or it wont set)

1 jar best quality lemon curd

200g + sugar

Melt butter and stir in crushed biscuits, press mixture into the base of a large, beautiful fireproof pie dish. Blend together cream cheese, fromage frais and lemon curd. Spread over biscuit base and leave in the fridge to set. (About 2 hours).

Once set, put oven grill on high, or you may use a blowtorch. Cover total area of lemon curd mixture with about 2mm sugar — place under grill turning frequently to caramelise evenly, or blitz with a blowtorch. Place in the fridge for at least 1 hour before serving.

This is lovely served with thin slivers of crystallised ginger.

You may want to make your own Lemon Curd:

75g castor sugar

Juice and zest of 1 large juicy lemon

2 large eggs

50g unsalted butter

Place zest and sugar in a bowl. In a separate bowl whisk lemon juice and eggs, then pour over sugar. Cut butter into little pieces and add to the mixture. Place the bowl over a simmering pan water and stirring frequently, allow to thicken. This should take 15 — 20 minutes. Cool before use

Chocolate Heart Cake

Valentines Day cannot be complete without a gloriously seductive chocolate cake to kick in the endorph
If you want to maximise this add a good teaspoon of dried chillies — it enhances the chocolate flavou
and doubles the rush! This recipe has real chocolate and a wondrous chiffon consistency.

225g at least 80% dark chocolate, broken
100g butter
2tbs castor sugar
4 large eggs
100g plain flour
1tsp baking powder
1tsp dried flaked chillies (optional)
Cocoa powder for dusting

For chocolate ganache
350g 80% + dark chocolate, broken
300ml double cream
½ tsp vanilla extract or vanilla pod if you have one

For white chocolate ganache piping (optional)
350g white chocolate broken
300ml double cream

Prepare a heart shape tin, line sides and bottom and grease. Turn oven to 180°.

Break the chocolate into small bits and place in a bowl over very hot water. Make sure it does n
overheat as chocolate will be unusable. When just melted, remove from heat and stir to smooth.
Beat butter and sugar together till pale and fluffy. Add egg yolks one at a time, beating well after
each addition. Stir in cooled melted chocolate. Sift and gently fold in dry ingredients. Add chilli
flakes if you are using them. In a clean bowl beat egg whites till they form peaks, then fold into
chocolate mixture. Pour mixture into prepared heart tin and bake for about 40 minutes till mid
springs back when pressed.

Leave in tin for about 10 minutes, then turn onto cooling rack, flip to keep cake top up.

Meanwhile, prepare dark chocolate ganache by melting chocolate in a bowl over very hot water.
Add vanilla to the cream and bring to the boil. Remove from heat. Remove vanilla pod if you have
one. Beat in melted chocolate and allow to cool. When cool, beat again using an electric mixer a
spread over the top and sides (if there is enough). Work fast as this hardens quickly. A spatula
knife dipped in boiling water will help if it solidifies.

Dust with sifted cocoa powder. Make the white chocolate ganache in the same way you have mad
dark. Place in a piping bag and pipe around edges and base. If mixture solidifies, warm up with
your hands.

You may wish to omit the white chocolate, the cake is just as delicious. Decorate with sugar rose
or violet crystals.

Enjoy with passion.

Baked Cheese Cake

Now the test of a true cook is create a baked cheesecake without the centre cracking in the oven. Generations of cooks have searched for a foolproof formula, but there is still no guarantee. At bes can suggest you do not open the oven at all during cooking, and leave the cake in the oven for or hour after cooking. Switch off oven and DON'T PEEK. Even if your cake does crack — it still is delicious and once cut on the plate, there is no telling how it came out the oven!

You can use a roll of readymade shortcrust pastry, but I'll give you the pastry recipe as it's eas and tastes nicer.

Turn on oven to 190°. Line a large Pyrex or pie dish with readymade shortcrust pastry or:—

Pastry

2 cups flour

1 egg

175g butter

1 tsp baking powder

Pinch of salt

2 tbs sugar

Rub butter into the dry ingredients and then add the beaten egg. Add a little cold water to create rolling consistency. Roll out on a floured surface and press into large pie dish. Mix a tablespoon flour and sugar together and sprinkle over base.

Cheesecake filling

1kg cream cheese

1½ cups sugar

4 large eggs beaten

4 tbs cornflour

250ml double cream

Mix all the ingredients together at a low speed till blended, don't over beat. Pour into prepared past shell and bake for 20 minutes. After this, turn off oven and leave in the oven for 1 hour.
Do not on any account open the oven door before time is up.

Good luck!

It does not need to be Shrove Tuesday to make pancakes. In our house they get made as often as time allows. Also, as they get guzzled as fast as they are made, I usually keep them warm in the oven — then we can all sit down to enjoy. The oven is no hotter than 100°, and if you place a sheet of greaseproof paper over the top pancake, they will not turn rubbery.

3 eggs

165g flour

Pinch of salt

300 ml milk

112 ml water

3 tbs olive oil or melted butter

Butter for greasing the pan.

In a large bowl, sift the flour and salt. Make a well in the centre, add beaten eggs and olive oil/butter whisk quickly till a stiff batter is formed, still beating gently add milk and water.

Heat a large lightweight frying pan, melt butter till sizzling and pour mixture into the centre, tilting pan around so it gets covered with a light batter — try to keep pancake as thin as possible.

When batter has set, flip pancake over and cook till golden brown. Place in the oven for warmth and repeat the process till all the batter is used up.

Pancakes can be served with lemon and castor sugar, oranges, jam and cream, golden syrup, cinnamon sugar, chocolate spread...... then there are the savoury fillings.

Pancakes

Pastéis de Nata

I would seldom begin a recipe with 'the real thing cannot be matched'. The competition is that of Belém in Lisbon, and the pastries are traditionally known as Pastéis de Belém. In the early 19th Century, many convents and monasteries were shut down. Looking for a way to survive, the nu~ were inspired to use the yolks left over from the dutiful starching of monk's collars into sinful l~ tartlets. Today, the wondrous pastelária opposite the Jéronimos Monastery churns out the same secret recipe devised by the nuns so many years ago (and this is why it cannot be matched, even today it is said only three people know the true recipe originated in 1837) but we try. The Belém pastelária makes over 14,000 pastries a day and pilgrims stand at least four persons deep to wait the pastéis to come out the ovens and be ready for selling.

I so hope I have not intimidated, these little pastéis deserve a try — good luck.

Part of the secret is a very hot oven — turn heat to 300°, or the hottest your oven goes.

1 packet ready made puff pastry

9 egg yolks

10 ml corn flour

500 ml double cream

150 ml castor sugar

Ground cinnamon and icing sugar to serve

Roll pastry thinly and cut into 14cm wide strips, roll into Swiss—roll like rolls. Cut rolls into 2 — 3cm wide 'wheels', and press into lightly greased patty tins. Refrigerate whilst making filing.

Separate eggs (you may consider making a batch of meringues with the whites). In a heavy bottome~ saucepan beat egg yolks, mix cornflour with a little milk or water and add to beaten eggs, add crea~ and sugar and mix well. Place over a low heat stirring gently till just before boiling point — the mixture should be thickening (not scrambling — if this happens remove from heat and keep stirri~ — it will become smooth). Allow to cool a little. With soup ladle pour egg mixture to ¾ of each cooled pastry wheel case. Bake in 300° oven for 15/20 minutes till centres almost blacken.

These are so yummy when freshly made and still warm.

Dust to taste with ground cinnamon and icing sugar.

You are a champion!

Chocolate Cherry Muffins

I usually need a chocolate fix first thing in the morning, and these muffins can sometimes be my excuse for satisfying the fix as well as having something vaguely nutritious to start the day. Please do not leap up at 5am to beaver away in the kitchen. I make a leisurely batch over a weekend and forage as I wish till they are finished.

1 large egg

½ cup sugar

¾ cup sunflower oil or melted butter

1tsp vanilla extract

2 cups flour

2 ½ tsp baking powder

Pinch of salt

1½ cups milk

1 tin cherries, drained and pitted

1 bar good chocolate — milk or dark to your preference.

Set oven to 200°. Line a 12 bun muffin tin with individual muffin cases.

Drain cherries and break up chocolate into squares.

Beat egg and oil together, add milk. Sift dry ingredients and add sugar. Make a well in the middle of the flour mixture and pour in the liquid. Stir just enough to moisten, too much beating ends up with rubbery muffins. (About 12 good circular strokes should do).

Spoon even amounts into muffin cases. Pop one cherry and one square of chocolate into each muffin (its ok if they poke out), and place in the oven for 15—20 minutes. Eat the remaining chocolate, have a great day!

A note on the cherry juice: It freezes well and can be used for ice lollies, or saved for adding to smoothies or sauces.

11

Scones

Scones are so easy to make and so delicious to eat — especially hot from the oven, with jam and lashings of cream! This recipe with yoghurt produces a wonderful light texture.

2 cups plain flour

3tsp baking powder

55g butter, cold

125ml plain or Greek yoghurt

1 egg

1 beaten egg (optional)

Turn on oven at 220°. Prepare a lined baking tray.

Sieve all dry ingredients into a large bowl. Cube the butter and with a knife, slice it into the flour for a bit. Now rub in remaining butter with fingers till crumbly. Beat together egg and yoghurt. Make a well in the centre of the crumbs and slowly add yoghurt mixture — using a sharp knife mix all together. If a bit too dry add up to 30ml cold water. When soft and spongy turn out onto floured surface and knead for a while, then roll out to about 2.5cm thick and cut into rounds with serrated pastry cutter, or roll to batons and using opposing diagonals cut into triangles. Brush with beaten egg (if desired) and bake for 10—15 minutes. Eat warm, served with your favourite jam and clotted cream for tea (or any other time).

Scenes

Marvellous Marble Cake

Marvellous Marble Cake has a true nostalgia; lazy afternoon tea in sunny gardens, cake on a cake stand with paper doilies, a china teapot and china plates with little silver forks..........

250g soft butter

250ml milk

3 cups flour

3tsp baking powder

1 tsp vanilla extract

2 tbs cocoa

1½ cups sugar

4 eggs

Pinch of salt

Chocolate glaze — see below

Turn on oven to 180°. Grease and line a springform ring tin or large loaf tin.

Cream together sugar and butter till light and creamy, then add eggs beating well after each addition. Sift in the flour, baking powder and salt. Mix in milk and vanilla till this forms a smooth batter. Mix up cocoa power into a paste using just enough boiling water. Divide the mixture in half and sti cocoa paste into one of these. In the prepared cake tin plop alternate spoonfuls of the vanilla and cocoa mixture till both bowls are empty. With a knife hastily crisscross mixture and bake for 1 hou

Once cooled a drippy chocolate glaze is added:

In a pot place 3tbs butter, 2tbs cocoa and stir over low heat till blended.

Add two cups sifted icing sugar and a beaten egg white — keep stirring till smooth and shiny, pou over cake immediately.

Finish with a sprinkling of chocolate vermicelli.

Enjoy!

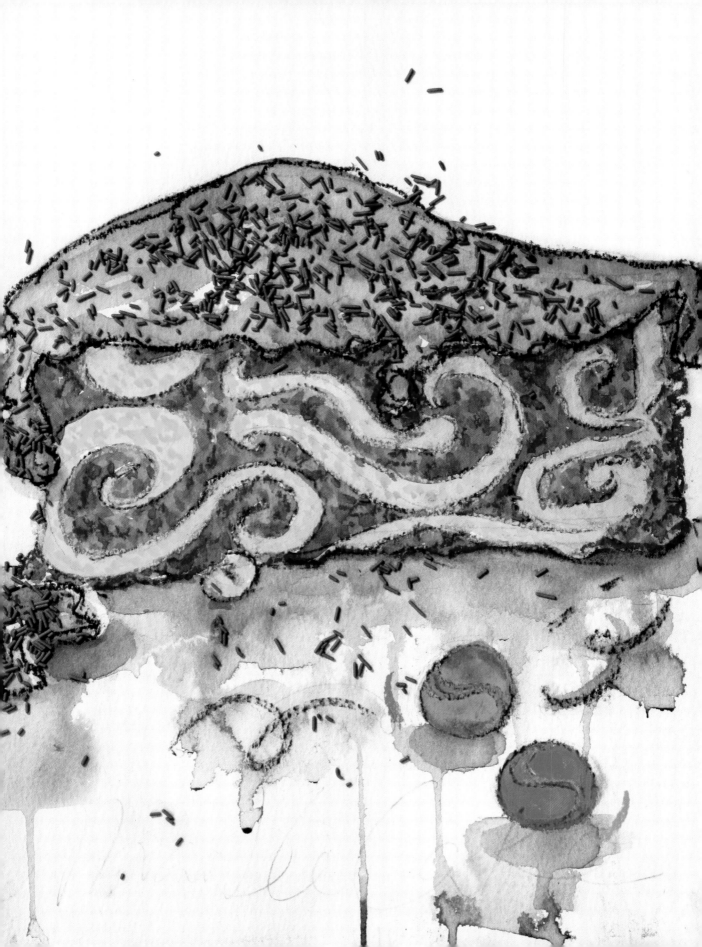

Banana Cake

Banana Cake is an excellent way of using up those pungent black bananas lurking in the bottom of the fruit bowl, you will need 4 or 5 depending on their condition — do slice away any truly manky bits.

4 to 5 ripe bananas mashed

Zest of one orange and one lemon

75g soft butter

110g golden castor sugar

225g flour

2 tsp baking powder

1 jumbo egg

50g pecans or walnuts.

Cinnamon sugar

Line and grease a loaf tin, and turn on oven to 180°.

Beat egg and then add butter and sugar, continue to beat. Sift in baking powder and flour and beat thoroughly. Lastly stir in zests, bananas and nuts.

Pour into loaf tin and sprinkle top with cinnamon sugar.

Bake for just under an hour till fully risen and top is golden brown.

Knife testing will not work as the bananas will be mushy.

Yummy as it is or with lashings of butter.

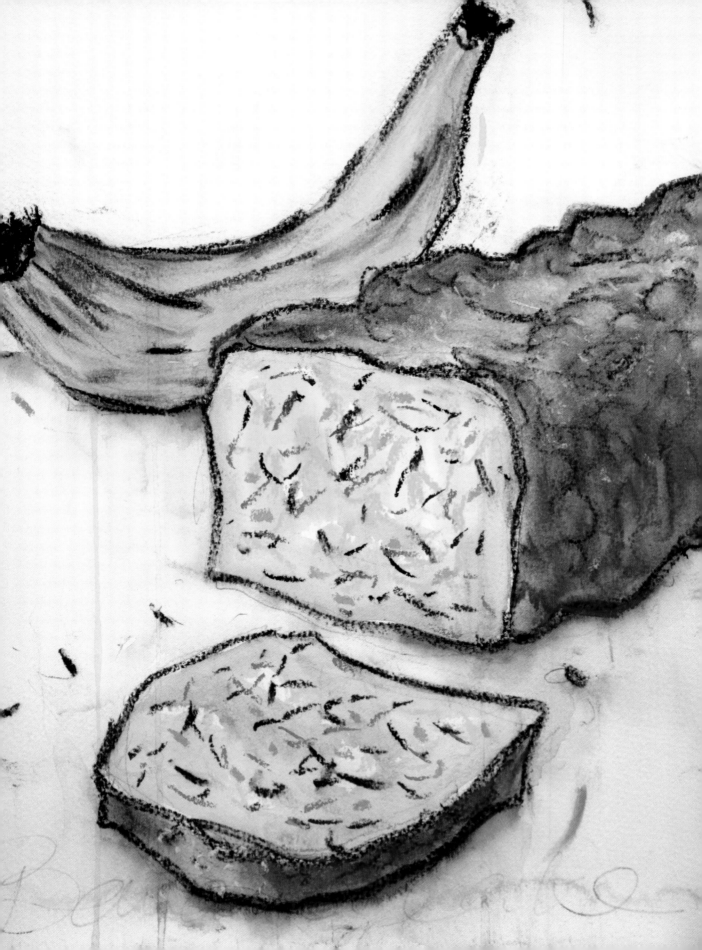

Almond Easter Cake

Easter is a time of Christian celebration and copious amounts of chocolate; it is the end of Lent and the rising of Christ from death. At about this time, the Jewish community celebrate Passover, another triumph over death and thanks for life. Whatever festival you are celebrating this wonderful almond cake originating from the Mediterranean will be well received by all — almonds being a Middle Eastern symbol for the awakening of Creation.

3 eggs

175g self raising flour

100g butter

225g castor sugar

125ml water

225g ground almonds

½ lemon zested

Some whole shelled almonds and icing sugar for presentation.

Turn oven to 180°, and prepare a beautiful 20cm pie dish or cake tin by lining and greasing.

Mix eggs, flour, water, butter and sugar together till very well blended. Add lemon zest and ground almonds and mix a bit more.

Pour mixture into prepared tin and bake for at least an hour.

If you have used a pie dish, cake can be served form this, otherwise tip out from cake tin and allow to cool. Decorate with a dusting of icing sugar and the whole almonds.

Is good for cake or a desert, if you have any room after all the chocolate.

These can be any biscuit recipe. Making cookie dough, rolling it out and using a range of cookie cutters is a riot. If there is anything left from either eating raw cookie dough, or guzzling the warm biscuits as they come out the oven, the real fun is icing. These Dalmatian biscuits have evolved to perfection and honour the memory of our more spots than brains Dalmatian; Dominique, or as my daughter called him — 'Doink'.

For the cookie dough

2 eggs

225g butter

225g castor sugar

450g flour + extra for dredging

1tsp vanilla extract

Icing

300gs icing sugar

Box of coloured icing tubes with red and black

Or small chocolate chips

Green or blue colour for the eyes

Silver sugar balls

Set oven to 180°. Prepare two baking sheets with silicone or baking parchment.

Cream the butter and sugar together, add in the eggs and vanilla. Sift dry ingredients and add to the eggs and butter mixture. If this is a bit wet to be rolled out, add more flour.

It may help to refrigerate the dough for about an hour, cover and cool. When ready, dredge a clean tabletop with flour and roll out dough no thicker than 5mm. Cut out shapes using a dog shaped cutter dipped in flour. You can use any cutter really and make up your own decorations, but if you are set on the doggy theme and can't find a cutter, make a tracing from one of the illustrations and redraw onto cardboard.
Cut out and grease one side — you can then trace out each shape onto the dough.

Cook for about 10 minutes and allow to cool.

Mix sifted icing sugar with about two tablespoons of water to attain a thick consistency. Ice biscuits and let the icing sugar dry. Dot with black tube icing or use the chocolate chips. Ice red collar and blue/green eyes. Lastly, press silver balls into the collar to make studs.

These end up looking too good to eat!

Woof.

Dalmatian bix

Flapjacks

Kids love making Flapjacks as they are fun and easy, lots of mixing, melting and tasting. They are a good portable breakfast and great for dealing with sugar cravings.

We always make a lot of Flapjacks and this is a big recipe, if it's too much for you, halve the quantities — but not the cooking time!

340g butter

220g brown sugar

110g golden syrup

500g rolled oats

Sesame seeds (optional)

Turn the oven to 190°. You will need two or three large pans.

Melt butter over a low heat. Add sugar and syrup and stir in oats. Dollop spoonfuls of mixture into the pans and smooth flat with the back of a large metal spoon. Sprinkle over the sesame seeds if you are using them. Bake for 20 – 30 minutes till golden brown. As soon as they come out of the oven, mark with a sharp knife into portion sizes of your choice. Once cooled and set, break and eat. These store well for a few weeks in an airtight container.

Enjoy the guilt free nourishment.

Mom's Lemon Loaf

Lemon loaf is always a winner. Use the freshest lemons available and do not stoop in using the squirt bottle variety, as it tastes bad and the plastic zest will melt in the oven.

75g butter

175g sugar

2 large eggs

200ml + milk

250g flour

2tsp baking powder

Pinch salt

2 large juicy lemons

2 cups sifted icing sugar

Put oven on at 180°. Grease and a line medium loaf tin.

Zest one of the lemons.

Cream butter and sugar together till light and fluffy. Beat milk, eggs and zest together.
Sift dry ingredients and add to butter mixture alternating with the egg mixture.
Pour into prepared loaf tin and bake for 30 – 40 minutes.

Meanwhile, cut a slice from the middle of the second lemon, set aside. Juice both lemons and strain. Add this to sieved icing sugar to form a smooth but not runny consistency. If too runny add a bit more icing sugar, if a bit stiff add a splash of water.

When cake is done and cooled, pour lemon icing over the top – sprinkling with a bit of zest if there is spare. Cut and twist the saved lemon slice and place in the middle of the cake. Slice to serve, lock all doors.

Red Wine Chocolate Cake

The best thing about this cake is that it has over half a bottle of red wine in it — meaning you have the other half left to drink as you merrily bake away. The result is also stunning as the wine flavour remains and blends seductively with the chocolate.

Cake

175g butter, softened

250ml sugar

2 extra large eggs

5ml vanilla essence

500ml flour, sifted

125ml cocoa powder, sifted

6ml bicarbonate of soda

310ml decent quality red wine

150ml water

Ganache

300g dark chocolate 85%+, in pieces

150ml double cream

Violet crystals for decoration

Heat oven to 180°. Grease and line one 23cm cake or donut tin. Cream butter and sugar till light and fluffy. Beat in eggs one at a time. Add vanilla and beat for 1 minute. Mix wine with water. Sift dry ingredients and add alternate dry and wine mixture together till a smooth batter. Bake for 50 — 60 mins (or till cake springs back when pressed in the middle)

Ganache

Melt chocolate slowly over boiling water, remove from heat and stir in cream — when almost cool spread over cake. Sprinkle with violet crystals if available for an ultra cool look.

En — hic — joy

19

mc the

Red Wine Chocolate Cake

Mousse Chocolate

The utter indulgence of a dreamy chocolate mousse is that it can be eaten at any time; my favourite is a few spoonfuls for breakfast accompanied with a shot of aromatic espresso. Use the best chocolate you can find and your freshest of eggs. This recipe comes from Lisbon and is made with continental ease in vast quantities just about every Sunday.

1 bar of good dark chocolate — at least 85% cocoa

6 eggs

2tbs butter

6tbs sugar, preferably castor

Flaky bar for decoration

This recipe is best made the day before as cooling helps to set the ingredients.

In a double boiler melt chocolate and butter till just runny — remove from heat and allow to cool.

Separate the eggs. Beat together egg yolks and sugar till pale and creamy.

Mix together chocolate and egg mixture.

In a clean bowl and using a clean whisk beat egg whites to stiff peaks. Pour over the egg chocolate mixture and fold together gently with a large metal spoon — at no time must any vigour be used or your mousse will turn to a slimy goo.

Pour into a serving bowl or individual little pudding glasses. Sprinkle with flaked flaky and cool in the fridge for the next day.

Serve with desert biscuits of your choice — continental chocolate wafers, brandy snaps or sponge fingers work well.

Thank you Deolinda.

Wedding Cake

I can't possibly give you a wedding cake recipe as most people have their favourite fruit cake recipe that has been in the family for years. Or you may wish to make a bottom tier of sponge, a middle tier of chocolate and an upper tier of fruit cake.

The bottom line in constructing a wedding cake is to have FUN. If you do not do paste flowers and intricate icing don't despair — you need a bit of royal icing piped around the sides and then ask the florist to create a trailing flower spray to your specifications. Give her your approximate cake height and a tracing of the cake tin you will be using for the top tier and she will do the rest!

My favourite is to place a fabby plastic bride and groom model on the top tier and buy paste roses for the sides.

The boiled fruit cake recipe is easy and can be made fairly near to the wedding date, depending on how much brandy you wish to spike it with. You will have to work backwards — two weeks beforehand it needs to be marzipanned and one week prior to the date it needs to be iced — either using regal or royal icing. The marzipan, royal icing mix and regal icing you can buy from any good cake supplier or even the supermarket.
If you are using sponge, chocolate and fruit combination — it will be only the fruit cake which will require brandy and marzipan.
The sponge and chocolate cakes can be made up to three days before the wedding.
You can easily tint the regal icing and I have previously used a grading of pinks which looks pretty. The colouring paste can be bought at the cake shop. It is also a good idea to use 4 dowels between the cake boards for support on the bottom and middle layers.

Shopping list for cake shop:

Enough regal icing

Enough Royal icing mix

Enough marzipan

Colouring paste

8 dowels

3 cake boards according to your sizes

Ingredients:

Boiled fruit cake. See week 38

Sponge cake. See week 42

Chocolate cake. See week 46

Brandy for spiking

Wedding Cake

Halva Cake

The creation of this cake came about by accident, and is a variation of the poppy seed cake which is very popular. Needing to whiz up a cake late one night I had all my ingredients mixed for the poppy seed cake and 'quelle horreur' I was out of opium seeds. Desperately ferreting in my store cupboard I was delighted to find a packet of Halva — voila! A new creation — it works really well as the halva melts and leaves a sesame toffee in the cake. For variation try pistachio halva.

3 cups flour

1½ cps sugar

4 eggs

1 cup orange or apple juice

1 tsp vanilla extract

½ tsp salt

4 tsps baking powder

250g butter

150g halva

Turn oven to 180° Prepare a springform ring tin by lining and greasing.

Add all ingredients to mixing bowl except for the halva. Mix well with electric hand beater. Flake halva with a fork and fold into the cake mixture. Bake for 40 minutes till baking aroma fills the house and cake looks brown.

Prepare to make many new friends.

Oat Bran Muffins

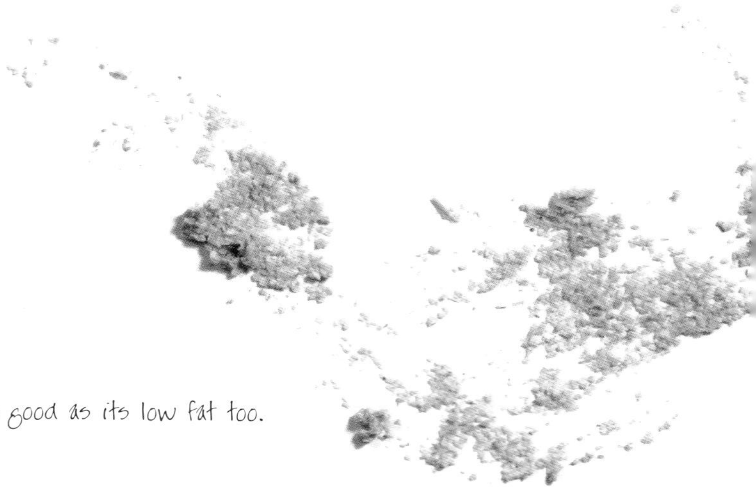

Another wheat free recipe, also good as its low fat too.

2 cups oat bran

2tsp baking powder

½ tsp ground nutmeg (fresh if possible)

1tsp ground cinnamon

1 cup skim milk

80ml honey

¼ cup sunflower oil

2 egg whites

1 cup seedless raisins

Turn oven to 220°. Line a 12 muffin tray with little cut out paper rounds not cases, and lightly grease.

Mix together dry ingredients in a large bowl. In separate bowl beat milk, honey, oil and egg whites. Pour onto bran mixture and stir just enough to coat the bran. Stir in raisin and spoon equal quantities into each muffin tin. Bake for about 20 minutes or till golden brown and slightly cracked on the top. Place on a baking rack to cool — don't forget to remove paper liners.

So yummy hot with a slab of melted butter, or honey drizzle.

Apfelkuchen

A very dear German friend gave me this recipe many years ago — we have since lost contact, but she remains with me through this wonderful cake she taught me to make.

200g butter

250g sugar

1tsp vanilla extract

3 large eggs

300g flour

Pinch of salt

1 tsp ground cinnamon

2½ tsp baking powder

100g chopped walnuts or other nuts

350g tinned or cooking apple, diced.

Turn oven to 180°. Prepare a 20cm springform ring tin by lining and greasing.

Cream together butter and sugar. Add vanilla and eggs beating well after each addition. Sift in dry ingredients and mix well, stir in nuts and diced apple.

Spoon into ring tin and bake for at least 45 minutes till edges of the cake separate from the tin.

This cake can be served warm with cream or ice cream and a sprinkling of cinnamon sugar

Wundebar!

Boozy Cointreau and Marmalade Cake

For lovers of Marmalade, not to mention Cointreau liqueur.

Do people still do afternoon tea? Well this cake is truly lovely after a few very thin cucumber sandwiches and a cup (china with saucer) of tea.

3 cups flour

1½ cups sugar

4 large eggs

1 cup freshly squeezed orange juice (about 2 oranges)

Zest of one orange

½ tsp salt

4 tsp baking powder

250g butter

1 tsp vanilla extract.

¾ jar marmalade of your choice

100ml Cointreau Liqueur

Turn oven to 180°. Prepare a donut baking tin by lining top and greasing.

First zest the orange and then squeeze to make up one cup.
Mix all ingredients (except for the marmalade and Cointreau).
Warm the marmalade in a pot and when runny, pour into the lined cake tin.
Pour over cake batter and cook for at least 40 minutes — till top is brown and sides are coming away from the tin. Turn out immediately — don't worry if the marmalade sticks to the tin, spoon out over the top of the cake and allow to dribble down the sides. When cool, place on serving plate and drizzle the Cointreau evenly over the cake.

This is delicious for breakfast too!

White Chocolate Cheesecake

I was privileged to be one of the finalists in the International Chocolate Festival held in Obidos, Portugal in 2003. This was a week of chocolate revelry with everything in the town dedicated to chocolate — sculptures, drinks, competitions etc. I was required to demonstrate the making of my cake to a TV audience and also have a cake for sampling. The queues for sampling stretched up the aisle and elicited two marriage proposals!

'Tho I didn't win (was tipped by pastry chef at the Barcelona Ritz), my judges were very supportive and said I needed a bit of contrast to make the cake more interesting — was advised to add tart fruit — fresh or in a coulis, but is totally divine on its own. Plain digestive biscuits also work well if you don't want to use choccy ones. It is a bit fiddly, requires a light hand but is definitely worth the effort!

200g dark chocolate digestive bix

90g melted butter

75g white chocolate broken into bits

200g full fat cream cheese

150g caster sugar

4 eggs (4 yolks, 2 whites)

568ml double cream

1 tbs gelatine

Chocolate for decoration — shavings or melted to be used for dipped fruit (cherries, strawbs...),

or perhaps sliced kiwi.

Prepare tin: 24cm spring form with sides and bottom lined with parchment.
Crush biscuits in processor and add melted butter.
Press evenly in bottom of tin and refrigerate.
Melt chocolate over bowl of hot water.
Whisk yolks, sugar and cream cheese till smooth.
Warm 100ml cream, remove from heat.
Dissolve gelatine in 4tbs very hot water, when smooth add to warm cream.
Mix gelatine cream into cream cheese mixture.
Whip remaining cream and fold in melted chocolate.
Fold with gelatine/cream cheese.
Beat egg whites till stiff and fold very gently into mixture.
Pour over biscuit base and refrigerate for a minimum of 4 hours, preferably overnight.
Decorate with fruit or chocolate shavings.

Gostar

White Chocolate Cheesecake

Jam Tart

Making jam tart is easy as pie, and I unashamedly take the cheats way out — bottle of jam and packet pastry. The fiddly bit comes when trying to lattice the top — this too can be overcome by owning a lattice wheel — it's done in one roll.

2 x 375g packets of ready made shortcrust pastry, thawed

Jar of jam of your choice, about 340g. Raspberry with pips is good

Fruit for decoration

Milk for brushing

Set oven to 220°.

Line a pie dish with the first packet of pastry, trimming as necessary.

Fill pie shell with jam to your taste.

Cut the second packet of pastry into strips, beginning in one corner lace two pastry strips across the pie. Continue round the edge till covered. Alternatively roll your prized lattice wheel over the flat piece of pastry and plonk it on top of the tart. Fork gently round the edges to seal the two pieces of pastry. Brush with milk and bake for 25 minutes, or when crust turns golden brown.

Serve with fruit and fresh cream. Don't eat when freshly baked as the jam retains heat.

Lemon Meringue Pie

If you are looking to save time, I suggest you use a ready made shortcrust pastry and concentrate on the filling and meringue. I love this pie just warm, but it is delicious to the last crumb at any temperature.

1 packet shortcrust pastry, thawed

25g cornflour

285ml milk

25g sugar

2 egg yolks

1 large lemon zested and juiced.

For the meringue

2 egg whites

110g castor sugar

Line a pie dish or deep flan tin with the ready rolled pastry, place in the oven and bake blind according to instructions (about 20 minutes at 190°). Allow to cool and turn oven down to 150°.

Mix the cornflour with a little of the milk till smooth. Add the zest to the remaining milk and heat carefully, pour onto the cornflour and stir in the sugar. Return the mixture to the stove boil for 3–4 minutes stirring constantly. Allow to cool.
Beat up lemon juice and egg yolks, add to the milk mixture stir till smooth and pour into the baked pastry case. Place in the oven for a few minutes to set. Meanwhile beat up egg whites in a pristine clean bowl till peaky, whisk in 1 tablespoon of the sugar and gently fold in the remainder. Pile on top of the lemon mixture covering up all exposed yellow. Sprinkle with castor sugar and place in the oven for 30 minutes till meringue looks set and begins to brown.

Eat when ready.

Chilli Slices

So yummy

So easy

So hot

225g ginger biscuits

50g hazelnuts

100g unsalted butter

185g 85%+ plain chocolate

2 tbs Golden Syrup

50g raisins

A brave pinch of chilli flakes

Juice of 1 lemon

Icing sugar

Lightly grease a sandwich tin or square dish.

Crush nuts and biscuits in food processor or in a plastic bag with rolling pin.

Melt butter, syrup and chocolate in a bowl placed over steaming water, stir constantly till dissolved.

Remove from heat and stir in raisins, chilli and biscuit mix.

Press into greased tin and refrigerate for a minimum of one hour.

This is yummy as it is, or you may want to add lemon icing:

Juice of one lemon mixed with enough icing sugar for a pouring consistency, adding a little water if necessary. Drizzle over slices and allow to set.

Sprinkle Sandwich

Am almost embarrassed in calling this a recipe — it's a family concoction, nothing brilliant, but has deep memories of pleasure, comfort and the delight of something pretty and delicious.

A sprinkle sandwich is just such — a dream, an indulgence, a treat after a wild day of activity or to the awe of classmates a yummy for lunchboxes.

It looks so pretty as well, my children could be persuaded to do anything when offered the reward of a sprinkle sandwich.

You will need:

Fresh white medium to thick sliced bread (you can use the white breads with added wheat germ to alleviate a bit of guilt)

Soft butter

100's and 1000's

Now here's the challenge:

Butter bread, sprinkle with 100's and 1000's

EAT.

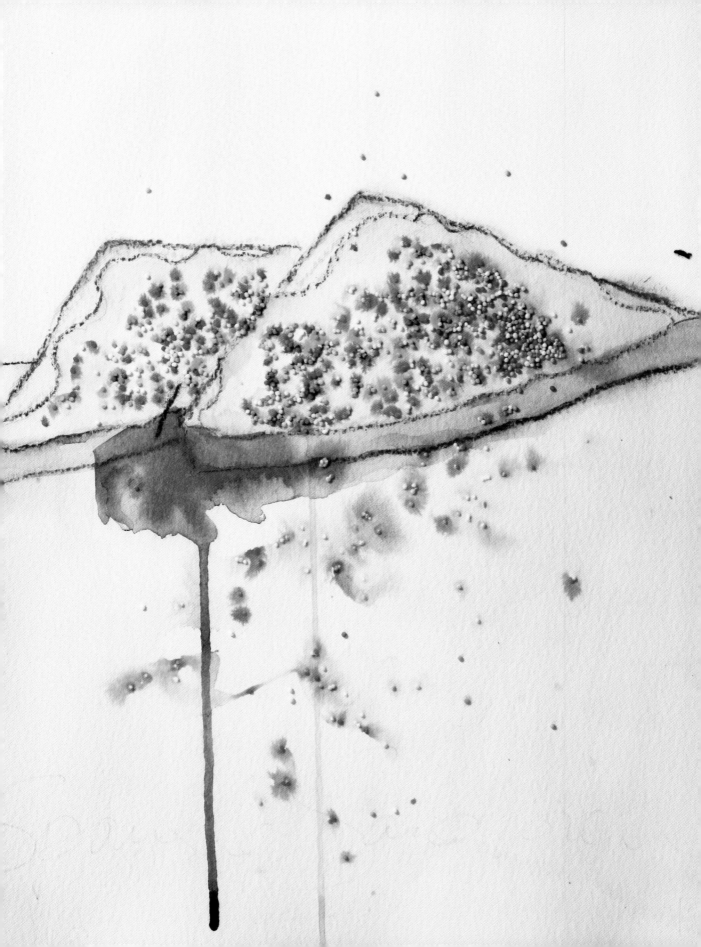

Broa Castellar

These unusual little Portuguese cakes translate literally as breads of the castle — they used to be made mainly over the Christmas period, but as they are so delicious, are now made throughout the year. The broas are not too sweet and keep for ages — in fact I prefer them once they are a few weeks old!

200g sweet potato (peeled, cooked and mashed to a puree)

110g ground almonds

110g caster sugar

2tbs flour

2 large eggs

2tbs corn flour

1 orange zested

1 lemon zested

Turn on oven to 210°. Line a baking sheet with silicone or baking parchment.

Mix together sweet potato puree, sugar and ground almonds over a gentle heat till moisture has evaporated. Cool and add one beaten egg plus the flour, cornflour and zested citrus. Mix thoroughly and then teaspoon the mixture onto the baking sheet. Flatten with a spoon and pinch each end to make leaf shapes, score along the centre. Beat the second egg, brush each little broa and place in the hot oven for 15 minutes or till golden brown.

Peanut Butter Cookies

This is a great recipe that children can make almost on their own as long as they are supervised with the oven. It is quite tough going mashing in all the peanut butter and unhygienically fun licking the spoon; tasting as the recipe proceeds, hopefully there will be enough to put in the oven. Bearing this in mind you may wish to double the quantities. American Peanut Butter can be bought in some stores — the abundance of dense crunchy peanuts makes this my peanut butter of choice.

75g butter

110g castor sugar

50g soft brown sugar

175g plain flour

1 egg, beaten

4 heaped tbs best crunchy peanut butter

1 tsp bicarbonate of soda

Pinch of salt

1 tbs milk

Turn oven to 220°. Prepare a lined baking tray using baking parchment or silicone. Beat together butter, castor and brown sugars. Add beaten egg and generous spoons of peanut butter, mix well. Sift in the dry ingredients, mix and lastly add the milk.

Place teaspoons of the mixture evenly on the prepared baking tray. Flatten each cookie with a fork and bake near the top of the oven for about 12 minutes.

Place on a cooling rack and eat whenever!

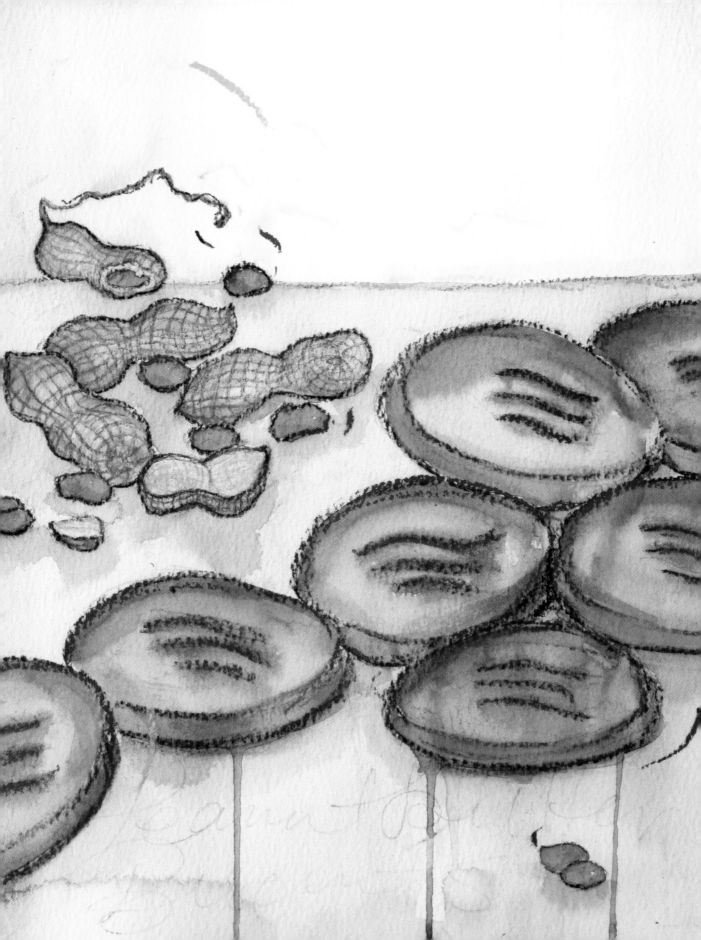

Birthday Cake

If you are serious about birthday number cakes, you may wish to invest in a set of number tins from 0—9. It may seem a bit wild, but once you have them birthday cake making is a doddle. Alternatively you may be able to hire the relevant number tin from your local store or bakery shop. This recipe will also bake well in two standard sponge tins — ice and pipe a huge number across the centre.

3 cups self raising flour

1½ cups sugar

4 eggs

1 cup orange juice (fresh or boxed)

1 tsp vanilla extract

4 tsps baking powder

250g butter (softened)

Set oven at 180°. Prepare tins by lining and greasing. If using number tins you will need to make a foil bottom. Tautly wrap a generous amount of tinfoil along the base allowing it to fold in place over the edge of the tin. The tin preparation takes the longest — now all you do is place all the ingredients in a large mixing bowl and beat till thoroughly mixed. Pour into tin and place in the centre of the oven. Bake for at least 45 minutes or when knife is clean as tested in the centre of the cake.

For the butter icing you will need:

150gsm softened butter

350gsm icing sugar sifted

Vanilla extract

Food colouring of choice

A bit of cream

Cake Candles

In a large bowl, mix together butter and icing sugar — add a few drops of vanilla extract. Add food colouring. If you are using a few colours separate into bowls first, or begin with lightest colour. Mix to a spreadable consistency and if too stiff add a small amount of cream.

Plaster your cake with a large flat knife and add some to the middle if you have used standard sandwich tins. Once iced, use a piping bag and large star nozzle to finish edges, write numbers or special message, plonk in some birthday candles.

Voilà!

33

Birthday Cake

Carrot Cake

It is seldom that carrot cake is refused, and once baked — this recipe will make friends out of your enemies, make best friends out of your friends and have mere acquaintances hug you with joy!

2½ cups flour

1¼ cups sunflower oil

1¼ cups sugar

3 cups grated carrots (about 4 whole carrots)

2 tsp ground cinnamon

4 eggs

2 tsp baking powder

¾ tsp salt

1½ cups pecans or walnuts, chopped (save a few whole ones for decoration)

Set oven at 180°. Line and grease tins — use 2 sandwich tins or a single ring tin.

Beat eggs and sugar well, add oil and beat again. Sift in dry ingredients, mix and lastly gently fold carrots and pecans ensuring a good coating and no carroty lumps. Bake for 40 — 45 minutes. As the carrots are moist, a knife test won't work here, but if your cake springs back when lightly pressed in the middle it is done.

For the icing you will need:

125g soft butter

125g cream cheese

500g sifted icing sugar

1 tsp vanilla extract

Beat butter and cream cheese together, add vanilla and icing sugar and mix to smooth consistency. Ice centre if you have used sandwich tins. Using a flat knife generously spread icing over the top and if you wish, sides of the cake. Decorate with pecan nuts.

Cancel your Rent a Friend subscription.

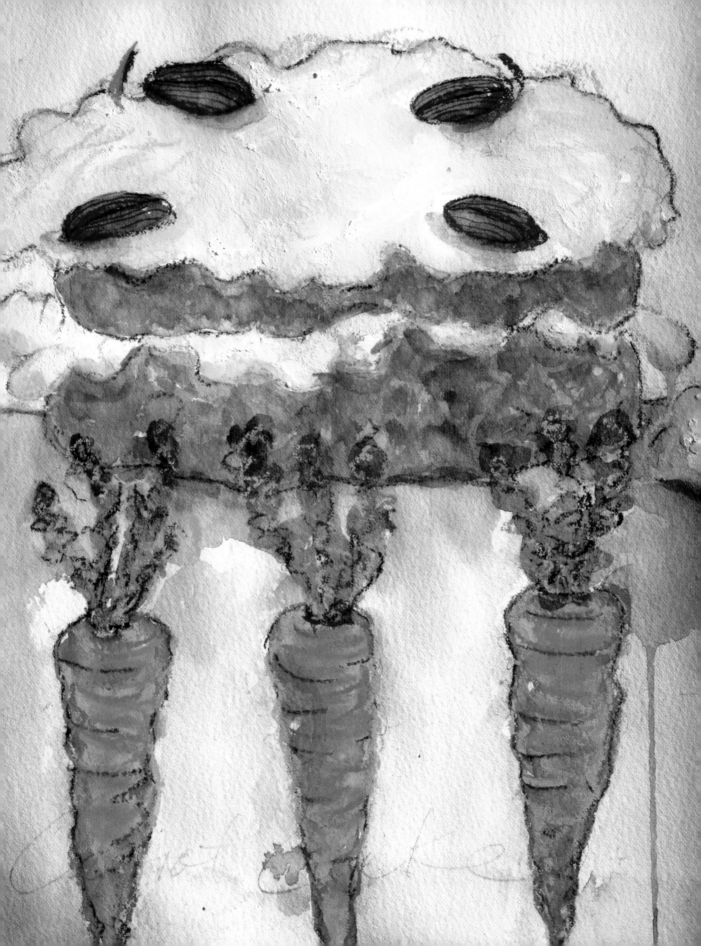

Shirley's Shortbread

Shirley loved to make shortbread, and we all enjoyed it too. This is one of the first things she taught us to make, always insisting on a light hand and NO finger licking

2 cups flour

2tbs cornflour

¼ tsp salt

75g sifted icing sugar

225g butter, softened

Set oven to 170°.

Sift dry ingredients, add butter (should be at room temperature) and rub it in gradually moulding into a soft dough. Knead well. Roll out in a circle to half inch thick. With a fork flute edges and prick dough's surface. Put on ungreased baking sheet and cook in very slow oven for 30 — 40 mins, till pale brown.

I miss you mom.

Ginger cake should have a tigers bite, in celebration of this wondrous root. The juices are supposed to help with motion sickness, and in China many women use a powdered form to help with morning sickness. In the Fifteenth Century it was used as a gift of love and respect and for warding off the plague.

The loaf keeps for ages and even better after a few weeks, served naturally with lashings of butter. The frosting is optional and the cake scrumptious with or without it.

250g soft butter

3 eggs separated

4 tsp ground ginger

1 tsp mixed spice or cinnamon

1 tsp bicarbonate of soda

120g dark brown sugar

2 tbs syrup (from ginger jar)

¼ cup water

500g flour

¾ cup milk

Pinch of salt

Prepare a lined and greased loaf tin, turn oven to 180°.

Cream together butter and sugar till light and creamy. Mix in egg yolks, syrup and spices. Sift four and salt and add this to mixture alternatively with the milk. Dissolve bicarb in water and add to mixture. Finally, beat up egg whites to soft beaks and gently fold into the ginger mix. Pour into prepared tin and bake for 20 minutes. Then turn down the over to 160° and bake for a further 55 minutes.

Frosting

2 cups icing sugar

Finely chopped ginger (either crystallised or from syrup ginger)

2 tsps ginger syrup

Water

Mix up icing sugar, syrup and enough water to make a dribbling consistency. When cake has cooled, spoon icing on top and allow to drip over the side. Decorate with chopped ginger pieces.

One of the things that is so English for me are the autumn months, big bramley apples on the trees and the brambles full of blackberries which are fun to pick as the days close in.

This is not a traditional crumble as oat flakes and a type of flapjack topping is used instead of the usual butter and flour rub. It makes a change and is also good for those following a wheat free regime.

3 — 4 Brambly Apples — you can use tinned if you need to

2 cups washed blackberries

Vanilla sugar

2 — 3 cups rolled oats

100g butter

1 cup golden syrup

Turn oven to 175°, select an ovenproof dish.

In a pot melt butter and syrup till runny — but not boiling. Mix in oats — a bit at a time till you get a good consistency and all flakes are coated. If it is too dry add a bit more butter.

Core and peel apples and place in cooking dish, add washed and drained blackberries and mix around gently. Sprinkle according to your taste with vanilla sugar. If you do not have any vanilla sugar at hand a jar of castor sugar which is shared with a vanilla pod works, or merely use plain castor sugar.

Cover the apples and blackberries with the oat flake mixture, pressing around the sides and into all crevices. This helps the oats to soak up fruit juices and adds to the yumminess. Bake in the oven for 30 minutes.

Glorious served with double cream, custard and/or vanilla ice—cream.

Of course you can use any fruit — plums work well too, but I love the apple and blackberry combination.

boiled Fruit Cake

How can any recipe be called this? It immediately sounds disgusting, but I was intrigued and delighted to find it worked really well — a good standby for wedding cake, belated traditional Christmas cake — or just for when you have the urge for something raisiny.

3 cups dried fruit — a mix of raisins, sultanas, currants, a bit of candied peel

1 cup sugar

1 cup water

225g butter

2tsp mixed spice

1tsp bicarbonate of soda

2 eggs, beaten

2 cups self raising flour

60g glacé cherries

60g mixed nuts

To Decorate (if needed)

Brandy — optional

A block of good quality marzipan

A roll of Regal icing or Royal icing mix

Cake board

Plastic Santa

Other

Place the first four ingredients into a large heavy bottomed pot and bring to the boil, stir regularly to prevent sticking. Allow to cool.

Turn oven to 140°. Prepare a 20cm fruitcake tin by greasing, lining sides and bottom and tying with string some brown paper on the outside. (The cake cooks in the oven for a long time and this helps combat burning). Make a brown paper top as well — cutting a small hole in the centre.

Once the mixture is cooled add all other ingredients mixing thoroughly — a heavy wooden spoon is ideal for this job. Pour into prepared cake tin and place in the centre of the oven, top with brown paper top. Bake for 4½ hours. After two hours have completed, turn cake around in the oven.

Depending on your timing you can consume cake immediately, or store it — with or without a soaking of brandy. To do this prepare a lining of greaseproof paper and a few lengths of tin foil arranged in a criss cross to completely cover the cake when wrapped. Take out all your frustrations by viciously stabbing your cake with a metal skewer or sturdy chopstick. Once cake is dead, evenly pour a cup of brandy over the cake to cure and wrap immediately, sealing all edges. This process can be repeated each week till seven days before cake is needed. If you like marzipan and icing do the following: Two weeks before serving purchase good marzipan. Unwrap cake, place on cake board and brush all sides with warmed smooth apricot jam or beaten egg white (to stick). Roll out marzipan over a dusting of icing sugar and cover cake — this is a two bit procedure. Trace top of cake tin to make top. For the sides make one or two strips using the side of the tin to measure length and width. Use your rolling pin to roll up strips and add to the cake. To seal use the back of a desert spoon to blend all edges — if you are regal icing smoothness is important. Do not cover. Allow to dry for one week. One week before serving either roll out regal icing using the marzipan method, or beat up a mixture of royal icing. The royal icing approach is to assume you are plastering the cake — a large spatula knife is used and finishing is either in blobby peaks or elegant swirls. In both cases to finish, pipe a line of royal icing round the base of the cake. Decorate with fresh flowers, plastic Santas or use your imagination.

Classic Trifle

Classic Trifle reminds me of huge family gatherings, drunken aunts, guffawing uncles, kids charging around and generations of love, laughter and bonhomie. It has to be the funnest and prettiest thing to make. I don't know where the advent of adding raspberry jelly to some trifles came from and you may include this if you wish, below however is the Classic Trifle recipe, with a splosh of extra sherry for the aunts.

Old bits of sponge, or make up Victoria Sponge recipe. See week 42.

Strawberry or raspberry jam

Custard in powder or ready made UHT form

500ml milk if you are using powdered custard

Tinned fruits — fruit salad, peaches, mandarins or fresh fruit

1 sliced banana

75ml sherry

Glacé cherries

Flaked almonds, toasted if you like

Sugar strands for decoration

300ml double cream, whipped

Select a lovely glass or ceramic bowl. Break up pieces of the sponge cake, spread one side with jam and place in the bowl. Splash with the sherry and add juice from tinned fruits if it looks too dry. Add the fruits. Repeat the process till all ingredients are used up or bowl is near full. Lastly add sliced banana. Pour custard over this ensuring all fruit is well covered. Top with whipped cream and decorate with glacé cherries and flaked almonds.

Sit back and enjoy the memories.

black forest gateaux

This wonderful cake is so dramatic — oozing with whipped cream, kirschdrunk cherries and copious amounts of dark chocolate shavings. It makes no apology for being indulgent, but if this matters it is wheat free!

6 jumbo eggs

150g castor sugar

50g cocoa powder

Large carton of double cream

1 tbs castor sugar

450g black or Morello cherries, pitted

At least ½ cup cherry kirsch

100g best quality dark chocolate or a flaky bar

Line and grease two sandwich tins, turn oven to 180°.

Drain cherries and set aside juice (you will need this later). Remove any pips. Arrange in a shallow dish and cover with kirsch — adding a bit more if you feel like it.

Separate eggs. Beat up yolks and sugar, sift in cocoa and gently fold.

Whisk up whites ensuring both whisk and bowl are clean, when peaked gently fold into cocoa mixture — pour into waiting tins and bake for 20 minutes till middle springs back and edges are separating.

When cool, drain cherries and save juice. Beat up cream, but don't churn it to butter. Stir in castor sugar. Add about two tablespoons juice to kirsch and sprinkle over cakes to moisten. Spread a generous amount of cream over one cake and dot cherries, keeping a few for the top — add grating of chocolate or flaky. Top with remaining cake and repeat cream, cherry, chocolate process.

Don't drive.

Dreamy Creamy Apple Cake

This one dish recipe is a good cake for pudding or high tea, it converts even those who do not enjoy cakes with soft fruit — and once again is dreamily delicious and easy.

For presentation, it helps if you have a beautiful oven dish in which to bake your Dreamy Creamy Apple Cake.

125g sugar

50g butter

3 eggs

125g flour

1 tsp baking powder

Pinch of salt

¾ cup whole milk

Large tin of pie apples

250ml double cream

125g brown sugar

Turn oven onto 180°. Lightly grease oven dish.

Cream together butter and sugar; add eggs one at a time. Stir in sifted flour, salt and baking powder and lastly whisk in the milk till mixture forms a smooth batter. Pour the mixture into a large, but shallow oven dish and plop in an even fashion the bits of tinned apple — don't worry if some of the pieces are not covered, the batter rises around them in the oven. Bake for 35—40 minutes. If you are serving this for desert, time your meal to finish after baking.

Meanwhile, over a low heat warm up cream and add the brown sugar, stirring till just before boiling (remove from heat when little bubbles appear at the edges of the pot), and the sugar has dissolved. Pour this caramelised sauce evenly over the warm cake — you can lift edges with a knife to let it seep underneath.

Yummy served warm and keeps well unrefrigerated for about two days.

For variety, you can use any tinned soft fruit; try plums, pineapple, cherries or even peaches — well drained of course!

41

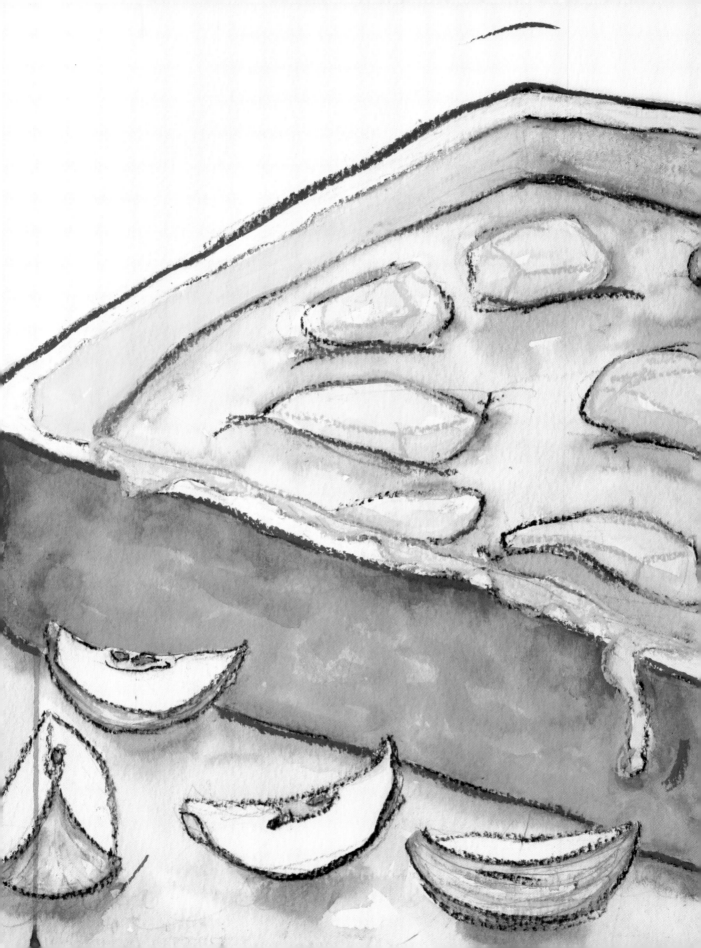

Victoria Sponge

Classic Victoria Sponge comes with nothing more than a dusting of icing sugar, plus a spread of jam and whipped cream in the centre. No matter what wonderfully exotic cakes you create, a Victoria Sponge will almost certainly please everyone. I like a huge cake, so if you think it may be too much, halve the ingredients for a flatter version.

220g self raising flour

1 tsp baking powder

220g sugar, castor works better

4 large eggs

220g butter — softened

1 tsp vanilla extract

20ml milk

Seedless raspberry jam

Beaten double cream

Icing sugar

Prepare two cake tines (18—22cm in size), by lining and greasing them.

Turn on oven to 175°.

Sift dry ingredients into a bowl and add all other ingredients, whiz up till fully mixed and divide the mixture into the prepared cake tins. Bake for about 30 minutes, till sponge springs back when pressed. Turn out onto a cooling rack.

When cooled spread a flat side of one of the cakes with raspberry jam. Add the cream. If you have beaten your cream so that it will not spread, randomly dot small amounts over the raspberry jam and then gently blend. Top this, flat end down with the other cake.

Serve on a cake stand if you have one and dust liberally with sifted icing sugar.

Just marvellous.

Briefly, this cake is to die for!
The cake has four parts to it, and I will list the ingredients in order of making method.

Meringue
3 egg whites
180g castor sugar
2 x 24cm rings of baking paper

Sponge cake

180g sugar
125ml water
200g butter
4 eggs separated
1tsp pure vanilla essence
120g self raising flour
1tsp baking powder
1 x 24cm cake tin greased and lined

White Port and Vinho Doce cream filling
3 egg yolks
110g sugar
75g flour
200ml White Port
50ml Vinho Doce (sweet white wine or champagne)
375ml double cream

Strawberry filling and sauce
60g strawberries
Juice of 1 lemon
A splash of White Port
Icing sugar for decoration

Meringue
Set oven to 140°.
Cut 2 baking paper circles using cake tin. (If you are sensible you could make three — one for the cake). Place on a flat baking tray. Separate the eggs in a clean grease free bowl, save yolks for the filling. Whisk the egg white till stiff. Slowly add in ½ the sugar till glossy, then sprinkle remaining sugar and fold into the mixture. Using a large spoon scoop mixture onto baking papers and with gentle circular movements smooth till level. Place in the oven and bake for about 50 minutes. Turn off oven. If possible, leave in the oven till cold or overnight — but no less than four hours.

White Port and Vinho Doce cream filling
In a heavy based pot whisk together yolks and sugar till pale. Whilst still beating, gradually add flour, then pour in White Port and Vinho Doce. Mix till smooth; if it is a bit lumpy use a hand blender. Cook over a low heat stirring continuously, till just below boiling. Pour into a cool bowl and cover with Clingfilm, cool in the fridge for a minimum of two hours.
Loosely whip cream and fold into cooled mixture just before assembling the cake.

Sponge Cake
Turn oven on to 180°. Prepare cake tin. Separate the eggs, whites into a clean grease free bowl. On the stove place the water and sugar in a large pot, heat till dissolved. Remove from heat and stir in butter till melted. Allow to cool. (Maybe at this stage you could begin the strawberry filling). Beat egg yolks and vanilla together, mix into the cooled butter mixture. Add sifted flour and baking powder. Whisk egg whites till stiff and fold gently into the cake mixture. When blended well, pour into the cake tin and bake for about 35 minutes, till spongy in the centre. After 10 minutes, remove the cake from the tin and cool on a rack.

Strawberry filling and sauce
Set aside the most beautiful strawberry, stalk and all. This will be used for decoration and needs to be fanned: starting at the bottom, make about four thin slices stopping just before the stalk, then gently fan each slice. Place half the strawberries (thinly sliced) in a bowl together with a splash of White Port. Place remaining strawberries in a blender and puree with lemon juice.
Mash through a sieve removing all pips.

assemble

whipped cream into White Port filling. Place cooled cake on a breadboard and
into three layers with a long sharp serrated knife. Start with a meringue base,
then add one layer of cake. Spread half the filling onto the cake.

strawberries, keeping juice for the puree. Arrange half the strawberries onto
filling. Repeat with the next layer, topping with the last round of sponge cake.
kle liberally with icing sugar, and place the most beautiful strawberry in the
le. Stir the sauce and strawberry juice in a jug and add to the cake on each
when serving.

se and die happy!

Super Chocolate Salami

One of the ultimate chocolate experiences — Is it a cake? Is it a biscuit? No! It's Super Chocolate Salami! Also easy to make and even easier to eat, this recipe is for two rolls, halve if required. Chocolate Salami is a no cook recipe, but needs to be made the day before so it can set in the fridge.

200g powdered drinking chocolate

200g very soft butter

200g castor sugar

200g crushed plain biscuits — digestives, petit—beurre or rich tea

2 eggs

Cream together butter and sugar, then beat in drinking chocolate. Beat up eggs and add to the chocolate mixture. Lastly fold in crushed biscuits — this should be a firm consistency, if not place bowl in the fridge for a while.

Prepare two large sheets of greaseproof paper, by dusting them with castor sugar. Divide the mixture into two and place mixture sausage like along the centre of the greaseproof paper. Wrap up and roll into a salami shape. Twist ends closed and place overnight in the fridge. To serve, cut into slices and keep cool till required.

This is another of my breakfast favourites.

citrus water sponge

This recipe is made light by water turning to steam, egg separation, and flour folding — all of which use hot air expansion as the rising agent. It produces a springy sponge in taste and texture, plus is made extra special with the inclusion of a citrus zest. Leave out the citrus if you prefer a plain sponge, substitute with a few drops of pure vanilla extract.

6 eggs

200g sugar, castor if possible

A heaped teaspoon fresh citrus zest — try lemon, orange or lime

50ml water

150g self raising flour

1 tsp baking powder

Salt

Turn oven to 180°. Prepare a large (preferably springform) ring tin by greasing and lining.

Separate eggs. In a large bowl beat egg yolks, sugar and citrus zest till light and creamy. Add water, beating continuously. Beat egg whites till stiff and glossy, and then fold them into egg yolk mixture. Finally, with gentle swooping movements, fold in sifted flour, a pinch of salt and baking powder. Pour into prepared tin and bake in the centre of the oven for about 25 minutes. When cooled, serve with a dusting of icing sugar.

Jen's Parev Chocolate Cake

Parev suggests this cake is ok to eat with meat meals as it contains no dairy.

I was originally given this recipe by a friend who follows a kosher kitchen, so the fat is a sunflower based margarine. I prefer to use butter in my cooking, which defeats the object, however I'll leave it up to you to decide which to use.

It also contains a glaze with egg yolk. You may want to be aware of the advice given to pregnant and older eaters to avoid raw egg, nonetheless I have to date not had any casualties.

This is a fun cake to make as it's made on top of the stove, plus the cake endures stabbing once it is cooked — great for little helpers or to vent some rage!

3 cups sugar

1 cup water

8 heaped tbs Bourneville Cocoa

400g sunflower margarine or butter

8 eggs

2 tsp good vanilla extract

2 cups self raising flour

2 tsp baking powder

Sprinkles of your choice

Switch oven to 180°. Lightly grease a large pan from which you will also serve this cake.

In a large heavy bottomed pot place water and sugar, gently heat till sugar has dissolved. Remove from heat and stir in cocoa and marge/butter till melted and all lumps are gone (sieving cocoa beforehand helps). Allow to cool.

Meanwhile separate the eggs. Beat yolks with vanilla. Whisk egg whites in a clean bowl till stiff and peaky. When cocoa mixture is cool enough add egg yolks and stir well. Remove a generous cup of this mixture and set aside till later. Mix in flour and baking powder. Gently fold in eggs whites.

Pour into pan and bake for ¾ hour.

Test for cooking by gently pressing middle of the cake — if it springs back its cooked!

When cool loosen round the edges with a knife and STAB cake with a skewer or chopstick. When perforated (or you feel better), pour over cocoa liquid that was set aside earlier. Ensure an even coverage, and also allow to leak down the sides of the cake. Cake will resemble a bird shot disaster — don't panic. Select your chosen sprinkles (sugar strands, 100's and 1000's, chocolate vermicelli) and sprinkle generously over the surface.

Enjoy

(Yummy big cake as it gets eaten so quickly)

Mini Pumpkin Pies

I'm always in a quandary with what to do with the pumpkin flesh that is scooped out when making Halloween lanterns. I hate waste and alternate between curried pumpkin soup or the following Mini Pumpkin Pies which are well received by troops of hunting Halloweeners.

1¼ cups cooked and drained pumpkin puree

¾ cup brown sugar

¼ tsp ground ginger

1 tsp ground cinnamon

Pinch of ground cloves

1 tsp flour

2 eggs, beaten

1 cup evaporated milk

2 tbs water

½ tsp vanilla extract

2 rolls ready made short crust pastry, thawed

Flour for dusting table

1 cup double cream

1½ tbs best maple syrup

Cinnamon sugar

Turn oven to 200°. Place 24 little foil pie cases on a baking tray. Dust a clean surface with flour and roll out the pastry to desired thickness. Using a pastry cutter cut out 24 rounds. Place and gently mould pastry to fit each case. Set aside.

Over a low heat cook pumpkin, spices and flour stirring continuously. Add beaten eggs, evaporated milk, milk, water and vanilla — do not overcook, this should be just warm with eggs beginning to set — not scrambled. Remove from heat and beat in the sugar.
Add spoonfuls of mixture to pastry cases and bake in the oven. Don't worry if the amount looks meagre, you will need space for the topping. After 10 minutes, reduce the heat to 180° and cook for a further 10 — 20 minutes till set.

Meanwhile you can make the maple cream topping: Beat up cream and stir in maple syrup. When pies are cool dollup a spoon of cream on top of each pie. Sprinkle with a little cinnamon sugar. If you are feeling creative, you could make parchment stencils of pumpkins, witches or spiders and sprinkle the cinnamon through these — stunning!

47

George's Glorious Jam Loaf

One of the great things about being a cook is that you meet other cooks and friends who love to cook. Over a coffee one can be solving the problems of the world when a recipe pops into the conversation and all interest is diverted to an intense discussion on ingredients, methods, visual presentation and the absolute yumminess of a creation. In some ways more immediately satisfying than the stuff that overwhelms us on a daily basis!

220g self raising organic flour, sifted

1 tsp baking powder

220g unsalted butter

220g caster sugar

2 goose eggs or 4 large free range organic hen's eggs

6 drops of vanilla essence

Best strawberry jam

Turn oven to 175°. Prepare a large loaf tin or two smaller ones, by lining and greasing all sides. George swears by the ready made paper liners that fit neatly into the tin — if these are used no greasing is required.

Put all ingredients into a large mixing bowl and whisk together till combined.

Simply spoon some of the mixture into the prepared loaf tin.

Add a couple of teaspoons of the best strawberry jam you can find and then repeat with more mixture and more spoonfuls of jam according to taste.

Bake in the oven for approximately 30 minutes.

When cool turn onto a wire rack.

You can finish the cake with a plain water icing if desired:

Mix icing sugar, water or add a touch of fresh lemon juice and drizzle over the cake.

This cake is received with great gusto as the local cricket team breaks for tea.

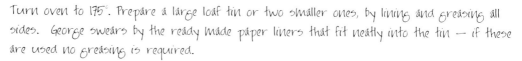

Marshmallow Crispies

I think the first thing I ever made successfully were Marshmallow Crispies. What struck me at the time was the sheer alchemy of throwing together ingredients to concoct something that nourishes body and soul. This recipe uses 6 cups of Rice Crispies, as to make any less is a waste of time and effort!

40 Marshmallows

3 tbs butter

6 cups Rice Crispies

Melt the butter in a pot and add marshmallows, stirring over a low heat till melted. Remove from heat and using a sturdy wooden spoon quickly mix in the Rice Crispies till all the Crispies are coated and mixture becomes stiff. Flatten into a greased baking tray or suitable non stick pan. When cooled and set, cut slices according to your needs.

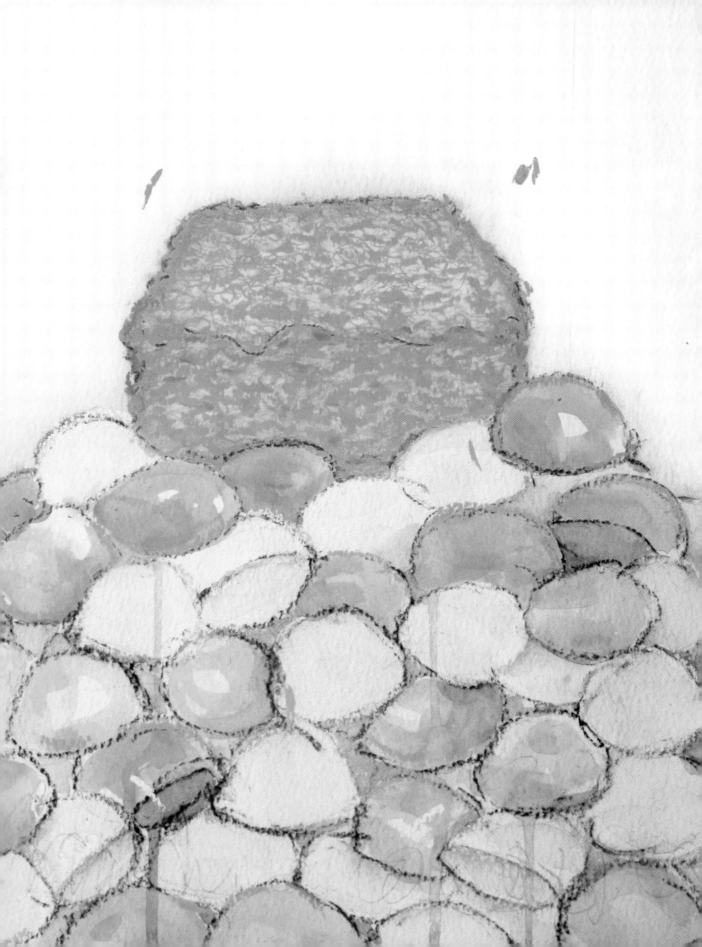

butter Iced Cupcakes

Cupcakes have been an obsession of mine for many years. They look so spunky and in decorating you can go to town, or be traditional with a cherry on top. I think why I really like them is that they bring out the kid in me. I never make less than batches of 24 and often loose control and churn out 48. The recipe is for 24, if you believe you need less halve it.

250g soft butter

250g castor sugar

4 jumbo eggs

250g self raising flour

1 tsp vanilla extract

For decoration:

325g sifted icing sugar

175g butter

Vanilla extract

Cream

Glace cherries, 100's and 1000's, sugar strands, chocolate vermicelli, smarties, sugar flowers etc

Turn oven to 200°. Line 2 muffin trays with muffin cases.

Beat butter and sugar together till light and creamy. Separately whisk vanilla and eggs, beat them into butter and sugar. Add sifted dry ingredients and fold till completely mixed. Spoon equal amounts into muffin cases and bake for about 20 minutes. I don't know if it is my oven or if this is necessary for everyone, but halfway through the baking process I turn the trays around, as this ensures an even cooking.

For the icing it depends on your mood. Sometimes it's good to make a thick water icing and decorate with halved glace cherries (Use a few tablespoons water to 300g sifted icing sugar).

Or make up a butter icing and sprinkle with 100's and 1000's, or other pretty things from your stash of decorations. Cream butter and icing sugar together, add vanilla and a few tablespoons of cream to help with the spreading.

If you are using 100's and 1000's with either icing, sprinkle after icing each cake, as the icing dries quickly and the 100's and 1000's end up bouncing everywhere!

Have fun.

Extraordinary Xmas Cake

I call this an Extraordinary Xmas Cake as it is quite different from the traditional — it has no icing or marzipan and so packed full of fruit and nuts there is little cake! It also looks extraordinary and I urge you to seek out a variety of fruits when making. The recipe is for one cake, but I make it by as many cake tins as I can fit into the oven. Dusted with icing sugar and wrapped in cellophane with a huge bow and perhaps a festive sprig of holly, they make stunning Christmas gifts.

375g mixed nuts (almonds, brazils, walnuts, pecans, hazels....)

100g dried apricots or figs (or a mixture of both)

100g dried, pitted dates

150g glacé cherries (multicoloured variety if possible)

75g raisins or sultanas, perhaps currants.

75g candied peel

1 lemon — zested, then juiced

75g plain flour

½ tsp salt

½ tsp baking powder

1tsp vanilla extract

75g brown or muscovado sugar

3 eggs

Turn on oven to 130°. Line and lightly grease +/— 20cm cake tin (if you are batching you may have a few sizes — what is important is the cake is not too thick).

Mix fruits, nuts, zest and peel together in a large bowl. In a separate bowl whisk eggs, vanilla, lemon juice and dry ingredients together to form a smooth batter. Pour over fruit and mix well with a large wooden spoon, ensuring each piece of fruit is coated. Turn into cake tin and smooth flat with spoon. Trickle all remaining batter over the fruit.

Place in oven to cook for 2 hours — if batching move cakes around the oven to ensure even baking. Allow to cool a little and ease out of tin by running the edge of a knife round the inside of the tin. When totally cold dust with icing sugar and serve or wrap beautifully in cellophane with a dramatic bow. The cake keeps for at least a month in an airtight tin.

If you prefer a traditional Christmas Cake use recipe for Boiled Fruit Cake. See week 38.

Pudim Flan

I sadly never met my mother in law; however she lives in our house by means of a large material bound cookbook published in the late 1940's. It is packed full of retro recipes and household hints, plus cures for most ills and social afflictions. Amongst these pages are also newspaper clippings, scribbled recipes and annotations on the results, good or bad. One of the things my husband loved most as a child was Pudim Flan, to my delight I found this recipe scribbled on a piece of yellowing kitchen splatted paper. Margaret calls this Pudim de Caramel; her children called it Pudim Flan. It is a version of cream caramel; I omit the lemon zest, doubled the quantities and guessed the rest!

4 beaten eggs

200g granulated sugar

2 tsp custard powder mixed with 100ml water

250ml condensed milk

100ml full cream milk

Turn oven to 180°. Fill up the kettle and boil water for bain-marie.

Select a dedicated donut mould tin or a Pyrex dish will do.
You may even consider individual ramekins.

Make caramel first by placing sugar and enough water to just cover in a pot.
Stirring regularly, heat till sugar dissolves, bubbles and begins to turn brown.
You will know it is ready when you can smell the caramel. This takes about 5 minutes.
Swiftly pour caramel into the mould and swirl around bottom and sides till well covered and sugar sets. In clean pot warm milk, condensed milk, custard plus beaten eggs and stir till it just thinks of thickening. Pour immediately into awaiting caramelised mould. Place this in a larger tin, to which you add boiling water, (your bain-marie helps to cook gently and keeps the oven moist). Place in the oven for 35—40 minutes, checking from time to time the water level. If this looks low add more boiling water.

When set, allow to cool and turn out onto a large rimmed plate.
Scoop out remaining caramel and pour over the top.

Thank you Peggy.

Notes

To view Burp The Movie,
visit www.everlastingcakes.co.uk